Table of Contents

Introduction:

Welcome, esteemed readers, to "Digital Horizons: Navigating the

Cryptoverse for Beginners and Beyond," penned by the cryptic quill of Maximilian Schmidt. Within these pages, we embark on a thrilling journey through the intricate realms of cryptocurrencies, blockchain technology, and the ever-evolving Cryptoverse.

In this age of digital transformation, cryptocurrencies have emerged as a beacon of financial innovation, promising decentralized power, borderless transactions, and new avenues of prosperity. However, venturing into the Cryptoverse can feel like embarking on an odyssey into the unknown, fraught with complexities, risks, and uncertainties.

Fear not, for this book serves as your trusted guide, illuminating the cryptic pathways, demystifying the terminology, and equipping you with the knowledge and wisdom to navigate this dynamic landscape. Whether you're a novice setting foot in the Cryptoverse for the first time or a seasoned cryptonaut seeking deeper insights, there's something within these pages to enlighten and inspire.

Join us as we unravel the

mysteries of Bitcoin, explore the quirks of altcoins, delve into the realms of decentralized finance (DeFi), peer into the future of blockchain technology, and discover the potential of cryptocurrencies to reshape our world.

So, dear reader, fasten your seatbelt, sharpen your wits, and prepare to embark on an exhilarating voyage into the heart of the Cryptoverse. The digital horizons beckon, and the journey begins now.

Chapter 1

Welcome to the Cryptoverse

A Beginner's

Odyssey

Hello, intrepid pioneers of the digital realm! Welcome to the Cryptoverse, a vast and mysterious landscape where codes replace currencies, miners are modern-day alchemists, and digital treasures await those with the courage to explore. In this chapter, we'll embark on a journey together, demystifying the basics of the Cryptoverse and helping you navigate this exciting new frontier.

Section 1

The Genesis of the

Cryptoverse

From the Ashes of the Financial Crisis

The Cryptoverse wasn't built in a day; it emerged from the ashes of the 2008 financial crisis. Enter the enigmatic figure, or perhaps group, known as Satoshi Nakamoto, who introduced the world to a revolutionary concept – Bitcoin.

<u>The Birth of Bitcoin</u>: Picture a digital phoenix rising from the economic turmoil. In 2009, Bitcoin was born, a decentralized digital

currency that aimed to bring financial power back to the people. Its creator, Satoshi Nakamoto, remains shrouded in mystery, like a modern-day Merlin leaving behind a magic spell for a new era.

The Blockchain Revolution: At the heart of the Cryptoverse is the blockchain, a decentralized ledger that records all transactions in a transparent and secure manner. It's like a magical book that everyone can read but no one can alter, making it the backbone of trust in this digital landscape.

Section 2

The Currency of the Future

Demystifying Cryptocurrencies for the Digital Dummy

Cryptocurrencies are the stars of the Cryptoverse, and Bitcoin is just the beginning. Let's break down the basics:

<u>What is Cryptocurrency?</u>: Imagine digital gold, but cooler. Cryptocurrencies are digital or virtual currencies that use

cryptography for security and operate on decentralized networks. They're not physical coins or bills; they're entries on a digital ledger.

Decentralization: Breaking Chains: Traditional currencies are controlled by governments and banks, but cryptocurrencies operate on a decentralized network of computers. It's like a financial rebellion against the central authority, providing financial freedom to the masses.

Mining: The Digital Alchemy: Mining is the process of validating transactions and adding them to the blockchain. Miners use powerful computers to solve complex mathematical puzzles, and in return, they're rewarded with new cryptocurrency coins. It's like turning digital lead into gold.

Section 3

The Cryptoverse Ecosystem

Understanding the Players in the Crypto Game

Now that you're familiar with the basics, let's meet the key players in the Cryptoverse:

Miners: The Digital Alchemists: Miners validate transactions, secure the network, and mint new cryptocurrency coins. They're the heroes of the digital age, turning code into currency.

Nodes: Guardians of the Ledger: Nodes are computers that participate in the blockchain network, validating and relaying transactions. They're like the vigilant gatekeepers of the decentralized kingdom, ensuring the integrity of the ledger.

Wallets: Your Digital Pockets: Wallets are digital containers for your cryptocurrencies. They store your private keys, allowing you to send and receive digital assets securely. Think of them as your digital pockets in the vast Cryptoverse.

Congratulations, brave adventurers! You've just completed Chapter 1, and now you're equipped with the foundational knowledge to explore the Cryptoverse. As we journey deeper, prepare for even more wonders, challenges, and digital treasures that await in this dynamic and ever-evolving landscape. Onward to Chapter 2, where we'll delve into the fascinating world of Bitcoin and its quirky companions!

Chapter 2

Bitcoin and Altcoins

A Crash Course for the Digital Dummies

Greetings, digital dummies!

Now that you've survived the initiation into the Cryptoverse, let's take a closer look at the two rockstars of this realm: Bitcoin and its quirky companions, the altcoins. In this chapter, we'll break down the basics, cut through the jargon, and get you speaking Crypto in no time.

Section 1

Bitcoin Unleashed

Bitcoin: The OG Cryptocurrency

Bitcoin, the granddaddy of

digital currencies, is like the wise elder guiding the crypto universe. Let's start with the essentials:

What is Bitcoin?: Picture Bitcoin as a digital coin with magical properties. It's not something you can hold in your hand, but it has real value in the digital world. It's like having gold in the land of ones and zeros.

Blockchain Ballet: Transactions on the Bitcoin network are like a dance performance – graceful, transparent, and recorded on a public ledger called the blockchain. It's the dance floor where all Bitcoin moves are showcased, and everyone's invited.

Decentralization Drama: Unlike traditional currencies controlled by governments and banks, Bitcoin is a decentralized rockstar. No central authority, no rules dictated by a big boss – it's like a rebellion against financial tyranny.

Section 2

Altcoins 101

Altcoins: The Quirky Cousins of Bitcoin

Altcoins, or alternative coins, are like Bitcoin's wild and eccentric relatives. Here's a snapshot of a few:

<u>Litecoin: The Speedster</u>: Imagine Bitcoin as a wise tortoise; Litecoin is the hare. It's faster and designed for everyday transactions, like

buying a cup of coffee without waiting for an epic saga to unfold.

Ethereum: The Smart Contract Magician: Ethereum isn't just a cryptocurrency; it's a platform for creating decentralized applications and smart contracts. It's like a crypto wizard, casting spells to automate agreements without middlemen.

Dogecoin: The Meme Coin Marvel: Inspired by a Shiba Inu meme, Dogecoin is the prankster of the

Cryptoverse. It started as a joke but gained a massive following, becoming a symbol of internet fun and tipping. It's like the class clown that somehow ended up being the prom king.

Section 3

Getting Your Hands on Crypto

Buying and Storing Your Digital Gold

Now that you know your

Bitcoin from your Dogecoin, let's talk about how to get hold of these digital treasures:

Exchanges: The Crypto Marketplace: Exchanges are like the shopping malls of the Cryptoverse. They allow you to buy, sell, and trade your digital assets. Choose wisely, though – not all malls are created equal.

Wallets: Your Digital Piggy Bank: Wallets are where you store your precious digital coins. Think of them as your digital piggy banks, but with extra layers of security. Hot wallets are online and convenient for everyday use, while cold wallets are offline and resemble a fortress against digital dragons.

Congratulations, digital explorers! You've just completed Chapter 2, and now you're equipped with the basics of Bitcoin and altcoins. The Cryptoverse awaits your next move, so go forth, explore, and may your digital adventures be filled with excitement and crypto treasures!

Chapter 3

Mining and

Minting

Unraveling the Cryptocurrency Creation Mysteries

Greetings, fellow crypto pioneers! You've now dipped your toes into the vast sea of cryptocurrencies, but have you ever wondered how these digital treasures come into existence? In this chapter, we'll embark on a thrilling journey to uncover the secrets of mining and minting – the magical processes behind the creation of your favorite digital coins.

Section 1

The Cryptocurrency Creation Myth

Bitcoin and the Genesis Block: Where it All Began

Imagine Bitcoin as the mythical hero of the Cryptoverse, starting its journey with the creation of the Genesis Block. Here's the tale:

Genesis Block Magic: In 2009, Satoshi Nakamoto mined the first-ever Bitcoin block, known as the Genesis Block. It's like the birth of a superhero – humble beginnings that set the stage for an epic journey.

Mining Rewards: Heroes need rewards, right? Miners, the valiant digital knights, solve complex mathematical puzzles to validate transactions and secure the network. As a reward for their efforts, they receive newly minted bitcoins. It's like finding gold coins at the end of a virtual scavenger hunt.

Section 2

Mining

Digging for Digital Gold

Unveiling the Mining Process in Layman's Terms

Mining isn't about pickaxes and hard hats; it's a digital adventure. Let's demystify the process:

Mining Hardware: Miners use powerful computers to compete in solving cryptographic puzzles. It's like having a digital race where the fastest solver gets the prize.

Mining Pools: Joining a mining pool is like forming a superhero alliance. Miners combine their computational powers to increase the chances of solving puzzles and earning rewards. Teamwork makes the dream work in the crypto world.

Halving: The Grand Event: Every four years, the reward for mining new bitcoins gets cut in half. It's like throwing a massive celebration, but instead of cake, there's a reduction in the supply of new bitcoins. This scarcity often leads to increased value – the Cryptoverse's version of a cosmic alignment.

Section 3

Minting New Altcoins

Altcoins and the Art of Coin Creation

Bitcoin might be the superhero,

but altcoins are the sidekicks with unique powers. Here's how they come into existence:

Forking: A Crypto Split: Sometimes, a community disagrees on the direction a cryptocurrency should take. In such cases, a fork occurs, splitting the original coin into two. It's like a superhero deciding to follow a different path, creating an alternate universe.

Initial Coin Offerings (ICOs): Cryptocurrency Birthdays: Imagine a coin's birthday party, where enthusiasts can buy tokens at the early stages of a project. ICOs are like crowdfunding campaigns that give birth to new digital currencies.

Proof-of-Stake (PoS): The Eco-Friendly Mint: PoS is an alternative to energy-intensive mining. Instead of solving puzzles, validators are chosen to create new blocks based on the number of coins they hold. It's like growing your crypto garden, where the more you have, the more you can harvest.

Congratulations, Crypto

Pioneers! You've just completed Chapter 3, unraveling the mysteries of cryptocurrency creation. Now, with a deeper understanding of mining, minting, and the genesis of digital currencies, you're ready to journey further into the heart of the Cryptoverse. Stay curious, and brace yourself for the adventures that lie ahead!

Chapter 4

The Cryptoverse

Navigating the Digital Landscape

Greetings, intrepid explorers! Now that you've survived the initiation into the realm of Bitcoin and altcoins, it's time to understand the lay of the digital land. In this chapter, we'll take you on a guided tour through the Cryptoverse – a place where blockchain technology reigns supreme, and decentralized wonders await your discovery.

Section 1

The Blockchain Symphony

Understanding the Backbone of the Cryptoverse

Picture the blockchain as the grand conductor orchestrating the music of the Cryptoverse. Here's the breakdown:

Blocks and Chains: In the blockchain, information is grouped into blocks, and these blocks are linked together in a chain. It's like building a Lego tower one block at a time – each piece connected securely to the next.

Decentralization Dance: Unlike traditional systems with a central authority, the blockchain is a decentralized dance party. No one's in charge; everyone's grooving together. It's the ultimate celebration of digital democracy.

Consensus Beats: Imagine everyone at the dance party agreeing on the same song. That's consensus in the blockchain world. It ensures that everyone in the network agrees on the truth, making it tamper-resistant. It's like a collective decision-making dance-off.

Section 2

Smart Contracts 101

Ethereum and the Magic of Self-Executing Contracts

Enter Ethereum, the wizard of the Cryptoverse, introducing the concept of smart contracts. It's like having a genie fulfill your wishes without the risk of any monkey paw mischief.

What's a Smart Contract?: Think of a smart contract as a digital agreement with built-in rules. It automatically executes when conditions are met, eliminating the need for middlemen. It's like having a contract that can enforce itself – magic, right?

Decentralized Apps (DApps): DApps are like mini-worlds within the Cryptoverse. They run on blockchain, providing services without a central authority. It's like having tiny ecosystems that function independently, yet harmoniously, in the digital universe.

Section 3

ICOs and Token

Sales

Raising Crypto Capital: It's Like a Bake Sale, but Cooler

Enter the world of Initial Coin Offerings (ICOs) and token sales – the Cryptoverse's version of fundraising, minus the awkward school auditorium vibe.

ICO Basics: ICOs are like crowdfunding campaigns, but instead of getting a T-shirt, you get tokens. These tokens often represent a stake in a project or future benefits. It's like supporting your favorite band's album before it's released.

Utility Tokens vs. Security Tokens:
Utility tokens are like tickets to a theme park – they give you access to specific services within a blockchain ecosystem. Security tokens, on the other hand, represent ownership in an external, tradable asset. It's like choosing between a day at Disneyland or owning a piece of the roller coaster.

Congratulations, Cryptoverse voyagers! You've just completed

Chapter 4 and are now equipped with the knowledge to navigate the digital landscape. Brace yourself for the wonders that await in this decentralized realm, where blockchain is the melody, smart contracts are the magic, and ICOs are the fundraising fiestas. Onward to the next chapter, where we'll uncover the secrets of keeping your crypto treasures safe and sound!

Chapter 5

Wallets, Keys, and Keeping Crypto Safe

A Dummies Guide to Fort Knox in the Digital Age

Greetings, crypto comrades! Now that you've got a grip on the crypto basics and understand how to ride the market rollercoaster, it's time to secure your treasures. In this chapter, we'll delve into the mystical world of wallets, keys, and the art of keeping your crypto kingdom safe from digital dragons.

Section 1

Wallet Wonderland

Your Crypto Piggy Bank: From Hot to Cold, Choose Your Castle Wisely

In the realm of crypto, your wallet is your fortress. Let's break down the different types:

Hot Wallets: Imagine a wallet that's always online, like a shop that never closes. Hot wallets are convenient for quick transactions but are more susceptible to cyber-attacks. It's like leaving your purse on the internet's busy street.

Cold Wallets: These are the fortresses of crypto storage. Offline and unreachable by hackers, cold wallets are like your secret vault hidden in the mountains. Perfect for storing your long-term treasures.

Section 2

Decoding Private Keys

Keys to the Castle: Guarding Your Crypto Kingdom

Now, let's talk about private keys – the magical passwords to your crypto castle.

<u>Private Keys 101</u>: Your private key is like the one ring to rule them all. It's a secret code that proves ownership of your crypto assets. Guard it like Gollum guards his precious.

<u>Public Keys</u>: Public keys are like your address in the crypto realm. Share them freely to receive crypto gifts, but remember, it's the private key that unlocks the door.

<u>Mnemonic Phrases</u>: Think of this as the spell to unlock a magic door. A series of words that, when recited in the correct order, grants access to your crypto kingdom. Write it

down, memorize it, but for the love of crypto, don't post it on social media.

Section 3

Safety First, Second, and Always

Tips and Tricks to Outsmart Crypto Pirates

Keeping your crypto safe is the name of the game. Here are some essential safety tips:

<u>Backups</u>: The Safety Net: Imagine losing your keys – not fun, right? Regularly backup your wallet and keep a copy in a secure place. It's like having a spare set of keys hidden in case you misplace the first.

<u>Two-Factor Authentication (2FA):</u> Extra Armor: Enable 2FA wherever possible. It's like adding an extra layer of armor to your crypto knight. Even if someone knows your password, they'll need a second key to get in.

<u>Beware of Phishing</u>: The Digital Hook: Don't fall for email scams or

fake websites trying to steal your keys. It's like fishing for crypto – except you're the catch of the day.

Congratulations, fearless crypto guardian! You've conquered Chapter 5, and now you're armed with the knowledge to keep your crypto treasures safe from the perils of the digital world. Lock those virtual vaults, guard those secret keys, and venture forth into the crypto landscape with confidence. May your wallets be secure and your crypto kingdom impervious to all threats!

Chapter 6

Navigating the Crypto Jungle

A Dummies Guide to Trading and Investing

Welcome back, fellow explorers! Now that we've got a

solid grip on the basics of Bitcoin and altcoins, it's time to dive into the thrilling world of trading and investing. Don't worry if the words "bull market" and "bear market" sound like a wildlife documentary – we're here to guide you through the crypto jungle step by step.

Section 1

Decoding the Trading Language

Trading 101: From Bulls to Bears and Everything in Between

Trading crypto is like being in a zoo of financial terms. Let's break down the jargon into bite-sized pieces:

Bulls vs. Bears: Bulls charge ahead, optimistic and buying up assets, while bears are more cautious, selling and anticipating a drop in prices. It's like a tug of war between positive and negative vibes in the market.

HODL: Hold On for Dear Life: When the crypto rollercoaster gets wild, some folks choose to HODL – a typo turned crypto slang for holding onto your assets, no matter what. It's the ultimate test of nerves.

FOMO and FUD: Fear of Missing Out (FOMO) and Fear, Uncertainty, and Doubt (FUD) are like the emotional rollercoaster of the crypto market. One moment, you're jumping in because everyone else is, and the next, you're selling because someone said the sky is falling. Stay cool − it's just part of the ride.

Section 2

Choosing Your Crypto Adventure

Investing Wisely: Where to Put Your Digital Dollars

Now, let's talk about how to choose the right crypto for you. It's like picking the perfect pet – each one has its quirks, but some might suit your lifestyle better.

<u>Research</u>: The Sherlock Holmes Approach: Investigate before you invest! Look at a crypto's whitepaper, team, and what problem it's trying to solve. It's like picking a superhero to join your squad – you

want the best.

Diversification: Don't Put All Your Eggs in One Crypto Basket: Just like you wouldn't bet your life savings on a single horse in a race, don't go all-in on one crypto. Spread your investments like a savvy crypto farmer planting a variety of crops.

Risk Management: The Safety Net: Set limits on how much you're willing to risk. Crypto can be as unpredictable as a reality TV show, so protect yourself from unexpected plot twists.

Section 3

The Art of Buying and Selling

Trading Techniques: From Novice to Pro in Three Steps

Now that you've picked your cryptos, it's time to learn the ropes of buying and selling. It's like playing a game of chess – strategic moves are key.

Market Orders vs. Limit Orders: A market order is like saying, "I want it now!" and buying at the current market price. A limit order is more patient, letting you set a specific price at which you're willing to buy or sell.

Stop-Loss and Take-Profit Orders: Think of these as your safety nets. A stop-loss order automatically sells your asset if it drops below a certain price, protecting you from major losses. A take-profit order, on the other hand, automatically sells when your asset reaches a certain profit level, ensuring you don't get too greedy.

Staying Informed: The Daily Crypto Digest: Read up on crypto news, join online communities, and follow influencers. It's like having a crystal ball that helps you anticipate market trends.

Congratulations, brave crypto adventurer! You've just completed Chapter 6, and you're now armed with the knowledge to navigate the crypto jungle like a pro. Remember, it's a wild ride, so buckle up, stay informed, and enjoy the journey.

May your trades be profitable and
your investments moon!

Chapter 7

Bitcoin and Altcoins

Crypto Magic for Dummies and Idiots

Welcome, dear reader! In this chapter, we're diving headfirst into the fascinating world of Bitcoin and its quirky companions, the altcoins. Whether you're a tech genius or someone who still thinks the internet is just a bunch of tubes, fear not! We're breaking it down for you in the simplest terms possible.

Section 1: Bitcoin Unleashed

Bitcoin Basics: Making Sense of the Digital Gold Rush

Picture Bitcoin as a digital gold bar, but cooler and without any risk of turning your fingers green. It's the pioneer of cryptocurrencies, created by an anonymous genius named Satoshi Nakamoto. No, we don't know who that is either, but let's roll with it.

Mining without Pickaxes: No, you don't need a helmet with a light on it. Mining in the Bitcoin world means solving complex math problems with computers, and miners get rewarded with new Bitcoins. It's like finding hidden treasures on the internet.

Blockchain Ballet: Think of the blockchain as a ballet of trust. Every transaction is like a dance move, and once it's done, it's recorded on a public ledger that everyone can see. No cheating allowed – it's the digital honesty policy.

Limited Edition Bitcoins: There will only ever be 21 million Bitcoins. It's like having a collection of rare Pokémon cards, but they're digital and worth more.

Section 2

Altcoins 101

The Altcoin Extravaganza: Bitcoin's Funky Friends

Now that you've got the hang of Bitcoin, let's talk about its eccentric pals, the altcoins. They're like the quirky characters in a superhero movie – each with its unique superpower.

<u>Litecoin: The Fast & Furious of Cryptos</u>: Litecoin is the race car of the crypto world. It's faster and lighter than Bitcoin, making it ideal for everyday transactions. Imagine buying a coffee with Litecoin – it's like paying with the Flash's credit card.

<u>Ethereum: The Smart Contract Wizard</u>: If Bitcoin is Batman, then Ethereum is like Iron Man with a side hustle. It introduced the concept of smart contracts, self-executing agreements without the need for intermediaries. It's like having a robot lawyer but less expensive.

<u>Dogecoin: The Internet's Favorite Meme Coin</u>: Inspired by a Shiba Inu meme, Dogecoin is the class clown of the crypto universe. Despite its meme origins, it's gained a massive following and even sponsors NASCAR cars. Because why not?

Section 3

Keeping it Simple

Wallets, Exchanges, and Keeping Your Crypto Safe

Wallet Wonderland: Your wallet in the crypto world is like a digital piggy bank. You've got hot wallets (online and connected to the internet) and cold wallets (offline and super secure). It's where you store your digital treasures, so choose wisely.

Exchanges: The Crypto Marketplace: Think of crypto exchanges like a shopping mall for digital currencies. You can buy, sell, and trade your coins here. Just be cautious – it's a jungle out there, and not all malls are created equal.

<u>Safety First</u>: Don't be that person who loses their keys. Your private keys are like the keys to your crypto castle. Keep them safe, write them down, and maybe don't tattoo them on your forehead.

Congratulations! You've just completed Crypto 101 for Dummies and Idiots. Now go forth, explore the crypto wonderland, and remember: even if you feel like an idiot, you're in good company. Cryptocurrency is for everyone, and there's always room for a little bit of magic in the digital age.

Chapter 8

Navigating Risks and Dodging Crypto Pitfalls

A Cryptocurrency Survival Guide for Dummies and Idiots

Greetings, fearless Crypto Warriors! As you venture deeper into the Cryptoverse, it's crucial to equip yourself with the knowledge to avoid the pitfalls and navigate the treacherous waters of the digital landscape. In this chapter, we'll unravel the mysteries of risks, scams, and common mistakes, ensuring you emerge unscathed from the crypto battlefield.

Section 1

The Perils of the Cryptoverse

Understanding and Conquering Risks

Cryptocurrencies, like any adventurous journey, come with their fair share of risks. Let's identify and conquer them like digital conquerors:

<u>Market Volatility</u>: The crypto market is known for its wild swings. Prices can soar to the moon or plummet to the depths of the earth. It's like riding a rollercoaster,

thrilling but not for the faint of heart. Set realistic expectations, strap in, and enjoy the ride!

Security Threats: With great digital treasures come great responsibilities. Be aware of phishing attacks, scams, and malware aiming to snatch your precious crypto keys. It's like protecting a castle – fortify your defenses with strong passwords, two-factor authentication, and a healthy dose of skepticism.

Section 2

Crypto Scams 101

Spotting Scams from a Mile Away

Cryptoland has its fair share of tricksters trying to part you from your digital gold. Arm yourself with knowledge to spot and thwart their nefarious schemes:

Phishing Ploys: Watch out for phishing emails and fake websites attempting to steal your private keys. It's like a magician's sleight of hand – they distract you while making your digital treasures disappear.

Ponzi Schemes: If it sounds too good to be true, it probably is. Ponzi schemes promise unbelievable returns, luring unsuspecting victims into financial disaster. It's like a siren's song – resist the temptation and sail away to safety.

Section 3

Common Crypto Blunders

Avoiding the Oops Moments

Even the most seasoned crypto adventurers make mistakes. Let's learn from the blunders of others:

Forgetting Passwords: Losing access to your wallet due to a forgotten password is a common crypto woe. It's like misplacing the map to your treasure chest. Write down your recovery phrases, keep them secure, and maybe tattoo them on your arm if you're feeling adventurous.

FOMO Trading: Fear of Missing Out (FOMO) can lead to impulsive trading decisions. It's like joining a frenzied dance party without knowing the steps – you might trip and fall. Stick to your strategy, resist the FOMO urge, and dance to your own crypto rhythm.

Section 4

Regulatory Risks

Navigating the Regulatory Maze

Governments around the world are still figuring out how to handle cryptocurrencies. Stay informed about the evolving regulatory landscape:

Compliance is Key: Different regions have different rules. Educate yourself about the regulatory environment in your area. It's like following the local customs when traveling – it helps you avoid unnecessary trouble.

Tax Implications: Cryptocurrency transactions may have tax implications. Consult with a tax professional to ensure you're on the right side of the taxman. It's like hiring a guide when trekking in unfamiliar terrain – they know the paths and potential pitfalls.

Congratulations, Crypto Guardians! You've now completed Chapter 8, your survival guide through the risks and pitfalls of the Cryptoverse. Arm yourself with knowledge, stay vigilant, and remember: in this digital adventure, caution is your most valuable asset. Onward to the next chapter, where we'll explore the future of the Cryptoverse and emerging trends that could shape its destiny!

Chapter 9

The Future Unveiled

Emerging Trends and the Evolution of the Cryptoverse

Greetings, Crypto Trailblazers! As we near the end of our journey through the Cryptoverse, it's time to gaze into the crystal ball and explore the fascinating realms of the future. In this chapter, we'll unravel emerging trends, cutting-edge technologies, and potential game-changers that could shape the destiny of the Cryptoverse. Buckle up, for the adventure is far from over!

Section 1

DeFi - The Rise of Decentralized Finance

Revolutionizing the Financial Landscape

Imagine a world where traditional banks are replaced by decentralized protocols and smart contracts. Welcome to the era of Decentralized Finance (DeFi):

<u>What is DeFi?:</u> DeFi is like traditional finance but without the intermediaries. It encompasses various financial services such as lending, borrowing, and trading, all powered by blockchain technology. It's like a financial playground where everyone has a fair chance to play.

<u>Smart Contracts in Action:</u> Smart contracts are the magic behind DeFi. They automatically execute agreements when predefined conditions are met, eliminating the need for intermediaries. It's like having a reliable butler executing

your financial commands with utmost precision.

Section 2

NFTs - The Digital Renaissance

Owning Digital Art and Beyond

Non-Fungible Tokens (NFTs)

have taken the art and digital collectibles world by storm. Let's explore the creative revolution:

What are NFTs?: NFTs are unique digital tokens that represent ownership of specific items, usually digital art, music, or virtual real estate. It's like owning a rare painting, but in the digital realm.

Blockchain as the Art Gallery: The blockchain serves as an immutable art gallery, displaying digital creations and certifying their authenticity. It's like having a gallery that can never be vandalized or robbed.

Section 3

CBDCs - Central Bank Digital Currencies

Governments Enter the Digital Arena

Governments worldwide are exploring Central Bank Digital Currencies (CBDCs) as the next frontier in the evolution of money:

What is a CBDC?: CBDCs are digital versions of a country's national currency issued and regulated by the central bank. It's like upgrading traditional cash to its digital form, opening new avenues for secure, borderless transactions.

Stablecoins and Economic Stability: Some CBDCs may be pegged to traditional currencies or commodities, ensuring stability. It's like having a digital coin that maintains its value in the ever-changing seas of the crypto market.

Section 4

Sustainability in the Cryptoverse

Green Technologies and Environmental Responsibility

The Cryptoverse is acknowledging its environmental impact and exploring greener alternatives:

The Environmental Concern: Traditional proof-of-work consensus mechanisms used in cryptocurrencies like Bitcoin are energy-intensive. Newer, more sustainable technologies like proof-of-stake and advancements in energy-efficient mining are emerging.

Green Initiatives: Projects and initiatives are focusing on sustainability and offsetting carbon footprints. It's like planting trees for every crypto transaction, ensuring that the digital revolution treads lightly on the planet.

Section 5

Quantum Computing Threats

Preparing for the Quantum Era

As quantum computing advances, it poses potential threats to existing encryption methods:

<u>Quantum Computing Risks</u>: Quantum computers could potentially break current cryptographic algorithms,

compromising the security of existing blockchain networks.

Quantum-Resistant Cryptography:
The Cryptoverse is exploring quantum-resistant cryptographic methods to stay ahead of the curve, ensuring the continued security of digital assets.

Congratulations, Crypto Pioneers! You've reached the final stretch of our journey through the

Cryptoverse. With emerging trends like DeFi, NFTs, CBDCs, sustainability efforts, and quantum computing challenges, the future promises exciting possibilities. As you continue your exploration, stay curious, adapt to new technologies, and embrace the evolution of this dynamic digital landscape. Onward to your next crypto adventure!

Chapter 10

The Cryptoverse Odyssey

Your Ongoing Journey and Final Wisdom

Greetings, Seasoned

Cryptonauts! As we stand on the precipice of concluding our journey through the Cryptoverse, this final chapter serves as both a reflection on the path traveled and a guidepost for the road ahead. Let's distill the wisdom gained, reinforce essential principles, and inspire you to continue your odyssey in the ever-evolving world of cryptocurrencies.

Section 1

The Ongoing Learning Curve

Adopting a Lifelong Learner's Mindset

The Cryptoverse is a dynamic ecosystem, ever-shifting and evolving. Embrace the idea that learning is a continuous journey:

Stay Informed: Cryptocurrencies, blockchain technology, and the broader financial landscape are in a constant state of flux. Make it a habit to stay informed through reputable sources, forums, and discussions. Consider it your daily dose of Cryptoverse news.

<u>Community Engagement</u>: Join communities, attend conferences, and participate in discussions. It's like having a guild of fellow adventurers who share their experiences, insights, and discoveries.

Section 2

Security Reinforcement

Guardianship of Your Digital Fortunes

Security is paramount in the Cryptoverse. Reinforce your

defenses against potential threats:

Regular Security Audits:
Periodically audit your security
measures. Update passwords,
review permissions, and ensure your
devices and software are up to date.
It's like checking the locks on your
digital fortress.

Hardware Wallets: Consider using
hardware wallets for long-term
storage of your cryptocurrencies.
These offline devices add an extra
layer of protection against online
threats.

Section 3

Risk Management and Mindful Trading

Strategizing for Long-Term Success

Navigate the crypto markets with wisdom, recognizing both the potential rewards and risks:

Diversification: Spread your investments across different assets. It's like planting a diversified garden – some assets may flourish while others weather storms, ensuring your overall portfolio remains robust.

Risk Tolerance: Assess and understand your risk tolerance. Crypto markets can be volatile, so set realistic expectations and only invest what you can afford to lose. It's like embarking on a quest with calculated risks.

Section 4

Beyond the Cryptoverse

Applying Cryptocurrency

Knowledge to Real-World Scenarios

The skills and insights gained from your Cryptoverse journey have real-world applications:

Financial Literacy: The principles of managing digital assets can enhance your overall financial literacy. Apply these skills to traditional finance for a comprehensive financial strategy.

Technology and Innovation: Cryptocurrency technology is at the forefront of innovation. Your Cryptoverse knowledge positions you as an early adopter, ready to navigate emerging technologies in various fields.

Section 5

Leaving a Cryptographic Legacy

Passing Down Knowledge and Values

Just as the Cryptoverse is passed down from generation to generation, consider leaving a cryptographic legacy:

Education: Share your knowledge with friends, family, and future generations. Educate them about the benefits, risks, and potential of cryptocurrencies.

Philanthropy: Explore ways to use your crypto wealth for philanthropic endeavors. Cryptocurrencies can be a powerful force for positive change in the world.

Congratulations, Cryptoverse Explorers! As we close the final chapter of our journey, remember that the Cryptoverse is not just a destination but a perpetual odyssey. Your understanding, adaptability, and curiosity will guide you through uncharted territories. May your digital adventures continue to be thrilling, educational, and filled with the promise of the future. Farewell for now, and may the crypto winds carry you to new horizons!

Appendix

Additional Resources for Further Exploration

As you conclude your journey through "Digital Horizons: Navigating the Cryptoverse for Beginners and Beyond," we've compiled a selection of additional resources to support your ongoing exploration of the Cryptoverse. Whether you're looking to deepen your understanding of cryptocurrencies, stay updated on the latest industry developments, or connect with like-minded enthusiasts, these resources offer valuable insights and opportunities for continued learning.

Books: Explore a curated selection of books on cryptocurrencies, blockchain technology, and related topics. From beginner-friendly guides to advanced technical analyses, there's something for every level of interest and expertise.

Online Courses: Enroll in online

courses and educational programs to deepen your knowledge of cryptocurrencies and blockchain technology. Many platforms offer courses taught by industry experts, covering a wide range of topics including cryptocurrency trading, blockchain development, and decentralized finance (DeFi).

Websites and Blogs: Stay informed with the latest news, insights, and analysis from reputable websites and blogs dedicated to cryptocurrencies and blockchain technology. These platforms provide up-to-date information on market trends, regulatory developments, and emerging technologies shaping the future of finance.

Forums and Communities: Join online forums and social media communities to connect with fellow enthusiasts, ask questions, and engage in discussions about cryptocurrencies and blockchain technology. These platforms offer opportunities to share experiences, exchange ideas, and stay connected with the broader Cryptoverse community.

Podcasts and Webinars: Listen to podcasts and attend webinars hosted by industry experts, thought leaders, and influencers in the cryptocurrency and blockchain space. These platforms provide valuable insights, interviews, and discussions on a wide range of topics, making them ideal for learning on the go.

Cryptocurrency Exchanges: Explore cryptocurrency exchanges and trading platforms to buy, sell, and trade digital assets. Many exchanges offer educational resources, tutorials, and tools to help users navigate the trading process and make informed investment decisions.

Regulatory Resources: Stay updated on regulatory developments and compliance requirements related to cryptocurrencies and blockchain technology. Government agencies, industry associations, and legal firms often publish guidance documents, reports, and whitepapers on relevant topics.

By leveraging these additional resources, you can continue your journey of discovery and exploration in the Cryptoverse, deepening your understanding of cryptocurrencies, blockchain technology, and the evolving landscape of digital finance. May your quest for knowledge be fruitful, and may you continue to explore new horizons in the exciting world of cryptocurrencies.

Glossary

<u>Blockchain</u>: A decentralized,
distributed ledger technology that
records transactions across multiple

computers in a tamper-resistant manner, providing transparency and security.

Cryptocurrency: A digital or virtual currency that uses cryptography for security and operates on a decentralized network, such as Bitcoin or Ethereum.

Decentralized Finance (DeFi): Financial services and applications built on blockchain technology that operate without intermediaries, enabling greater access, transparency, and efficiency in the financial system.

Digital Wallet: Software or hardware used to store, manage, and transact with cryptocurrencies, allowing users to securely store their private keys and access their digital assets.

Fiat Currency: Government-issued currency that is not backed by a physical commodity but has value because the government maintains its use as a medium of exchange, such as the US dollar or Euro.

Mining: The process of validating and adding transactions to a blockchain by solving complex mathematical puzzles, typically associated with the creation of new cryptocurrency coins.

Non-Fungible Token (NFT): A unique digital asset stored on a blockchain that represents ownership of a specific item, such as digital art, collectibles, or virtual real estate.

Private Key: A cryptographic key used to access and control a user's cryptocurrency holdings, providing ownership and authorization for transactions.

Smart Contract: Self-executing contracts with the terms of the agreement directly written into code, automatically executing actions when predefined conditions are met on a blockchain.

Token: A digital representation of an asset or utility stored on a blockchain, often used in decentralized applications (DApps) and tokenized assets.

<u>Wallet Address</u>: A unique identifier associated with a digital wallet, used to send and receive cryptocurrencies on a blockchain network.

These definitions are provided as a reference to assist readers in understanding key terms and concepts related to cryptocurrencies and blockchain technology. As the industry evolves, new terms may emerge, and existing definitions may evolve.

Farewell to the Cryptoverse, Until We Meet Again

As we draw the curtains on our journey through the Cryptoverse, it's time to reflect on the knowledge gained, the adventures shared, and the horizons yet to be explored. In this conclusion, we bid adieu to the Cryptoverse, but not without a heartfelt farewell and a promise of future rendezvous.

Throughout this book, we've traversed the digital landscape, from the humble beginnings of Bitcoin to the cutting-edge innovations shaping the future of finance. We've demystified the complexities of blockchain technology, navigated the risks and pitfalls of the Cryptoverse, and envisioned the possibilities of emerging trends like decentralized finance and non-fungible tokens.

But our journey doesn't end here; it merely takes a brief pause. The Cryptoverse is a dynamic and ever-evolving realm, where new discoveries await and new adventures beckon. As you close this book, remember that the knowledge and insights you've gained are your compass, guiding you through the twists and turns of this digital odyssey.

So, dear reader, as you bid farewell to the Cryptoverse, carry with you the lessons learned, the wisdom acquired, and the curiosity that fuels exploration. Keep your eyes on the digital horizons, for they hold the promise of a future where decentralized possibilities are limitless, and the journey is as rewarding as the destination.

Until we meet again in the vast expanse of the Cryptoverse, farewell, and may your adventures be filled with discovery, growth, and boundless opportunities.